MW01172600

Stop Hitting Snooze At The Sound Of Your Alarm

This Book Is Proudly Published

By

Write That Book Now Publishing

Stop hitting snooze: What is it about?

Touching on topics of reality, sharing stories.

Providing resources for further interest/growth/development.

Providing another access point of information to those who otherwise would not get it.

The starting point to something greater.

Forward

My alarm: My snooze: My story

I finally hit the snooze and woke up out of the fog of my own existence when I resigned from a job that I had been working at for 5 years, 2 years post my graduate degree, and in that time, only received cost of living raises. There were other parts to the story. Personally. Professionally, Academically……….

I resigned with a credit score in the 500's. Two of my children were in college. My youngest was heading to high school. All of my bills were late…..ALLLLL OF THEM. No interviews for another job insight. No residual income to count on. No husband to count on. JUST FAITH and GOD's reassurance.

I was the UBER Lady….I started driving with the hopes of saving money, then using the money to pay my car note, then the reality…I was driving just to put dinner on the table, putting 10 in the tank to drive to earn 30 to get me through the week. Being the UBER Lady for the short time that I was, allowed me to be able to hear God's voice through those I drove from place to place. I was able to sit still with someone as he spoke to me through them. I was able to minister to some while others ministered to me. In between pick-ups, I was able to minister to myself and embrace what blessings were in my lap.

I knew I had to leave my current employment situation. I was not under the proper leadership for me as I was not being challenged. I was not leading at the capability that I was called to do; I was settling. I was losing self-esteem. I was holding on to a battle that I fought long ago….and won. I worked with students who relied on the Department of Public Welfare to supplement their funding with SNAP and or TANF benefits while attending school and trying to make an upgrade for them and their families. I was who I needed to be when I was at the same stage they were in now. I was so blinded by being for them what I needed, so I became one of them (struggling to make ends meet, doubting my capabilities, relying on others just to get by). I can hear a voice from a public figure saying, "My dad said son, the only way to help poor people is to not be one of them" (Steve Harvey). So, I realized…If I truly want to help first-generation, non-traditional, single-parent, check to check individuals change the trajectory of their life…. I had to be willing to change mine.

I am a LEGACY Junkie. I want to leave a legacy that empowers generations. If that was my plan… I needed to do something quick, drastic, bold, faithful. I did, I QUIT! Not just my job…. I QUIT doubting, complaining, settling, struggling, dozing off, and avoiding.

Leaving this job was like leaving a relationship. It was no longer benefiting me and I was pouring too much into it with little return.

My snooze was about getting out of the mind frame that I had set myself in a quarter of a century ago. I was a young mother whose decisions put her in a place where she felt less than and deserved a hard way to go. I put my child first and lived through how I was a mother to him. My decisions forced him to reap the consequences. I parented out of guilt, desperation, and shame. I attempted to look the part on the outside, deflect from what I was really battling, helping others at all cost while unknowingly silently SCREAMING for help. When you get into a cycle, you lose sight of what your journey is…. I did that, not for days, weeks, months or years…but decades. I was wasting the gift that GOD created in me.

As a result of my actions to stop hitting snooze….I was able to produce this book, start a small business, create ideas for a nonprofit, witness two of my children graduate college, and embrace who I am; flaws and all.

So now, get started on how you will stop hitting that snooze button at the sound of your alarm!

Table of Contents

Mind

Body

Soul

MIND

(Recall and use of unconscious mind; bad information; what do we tell ourselves)

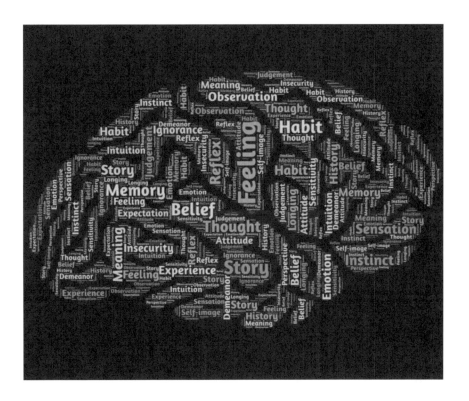

Chapter 1

Death By Incarceration:

There is an infestation of doubt and shame that needs to be eradicated:

Picture it, you are in your thirties and you recall a time when you were not double digits yet. You see yourself in a situation that you have/had no control over, you were helpless and the adults in your life failed you miserably (unintentionally but nevertheless, you were abandoned at that moment). It could have been your parent, neighbor, coach, teacher doctor or just an adult that had the capability of intervening and did not. How did you feel? What do you tell yourself? How did it affect your future? RELEASE the shackles of what was and live for now. Make sure you heal that inner child and be vigilant that another child does not have the same experience on your watch. This is easier said than done, but like Iyanla Vanzant says, "You need to do the work beloved!" It is time to be SELF-disciplined.

According to Merriam Webster's dictionary, self-discipline is the correction or regulation of oneself for the sake of improvement. The Cambridge Dictionary indicates that self-discipline is the ability to make yourself do things you know you should do even when you do not want to.

Write out 3 things that you have attempted to do in the past that you know you needed to have been self-disciplined but failed

1. _____

2. _____

3. _____

What could you have done differently? Did you set SMART Goals? When you realized you failed or gave up, what did it reaffirm for you? Now imagine if you succeeded, how would you have felt? Going forward, you need to incorporate these three main ingredients: Commitment, focus and persistence.

Probably the most common scenario is weight loss. You catch a glimpse of yourself in the mirror one day when drying off from a shower; you do a double-take and see one, two, no three rolls between your shoulder blade and your lower back, and from that moment on, you vow to lose 15 to 20 lbs. You download exercise and calorie counting apps, then buy a gym membership and some workout clothes. You update your playlist and buy an expensive water bottle. You're ready; you set yourself up for success with quick references, you look cute, you surround yourself around others with the same plan. Then the elliptical takes the breath out of your chest and inserts jelly where your leg muscles used to be. You quickly think about what undergarments and new clothing trends you can get to camouflage your "trouble" areas. Where is the self-discipline when you hit a wall or look up and see the ascend of the mountain! Self-discipline needs to partner with goals, SMART (attachment in appendix) goals to be exact. Goals need to be Specific, Measurable, Attainable, Realistic and Timed. So, let's double back; the goal is to lose 15-20 lbs. (specific) you can say that you are going to walk for 30 min a day (time) for a week and not only weigh yourself but measure your waist as well (measurable). You then decide that you want to focus on losing 2-3 pounds per week over a 6-8-week period. (Realistic) You can add on a new activity or restrictions weekly (Attainable) such as drink more water week 1, walk 5 min longer week 2, eat less carbs week 3, add running week 4, count calories week 5, add weights week 6, etc.

I spoke with a young lady who recently passed her NCLEX exam to become a Registered Nurse. She attended a college that was known for its academics as well as being a party school. I asked her how she was able to complete her degree in four years; how did you maintain your focus? She indicated that she put her goal BSN Bachelor of Science in Nursing on her wall in her dorm and every semester she would make sure she had smaller goals visible as well as chart what she did daily that supported her attaining her goals (short term and or long term). Knowing that sometimes you can't do it alone, she surrounded herself with others that were like-minded, so she became close friends with other nursing students who also graduated within a four-year time frame. While practicing self-discipline and incorporating a support system, they saw that with hard work comes reward. They would plan their week around celebrating on Tuesdays at a local club that offered discounted meals at happy hour, practicing self-discipline, understanding delayed gratification and being financially savvy was a part of their everyday life for four years.

Some people have an issue with shame that keeps them in the cell of their past, break free and live. You need to confide in someone that you trust to hold you accountable as well as be your cheerleader. Shame allows others to tell your story, take your power back and use your shame/experiences as a platform to save, encourage and hold others accountable. There was a young man in his twenties who thought he was worthless because he had 4 children by 4 different women. The first three relationships, he was an abuser. His firstborn, his only son, was born on his 17th birthday to a 15-year-old mother. He was emotionally abusive by secluding her from family and friends and demeaning her in private and public. His first daughter was born a year and two months later to an older woman with two other children. He was financially abusive by keeping her on a string and providing her housing and gifts as he had become a local drug dealer with charisma and fearless intent to get what he wanted. Dealing drugs exposes you to the lifestyle, so he began to sample his product and drink. Six months later came another daughter; her mother was just as fearless and feisty. The combination led to a physically abusive relationship on both parts. Typically, the abuse was initiated by her, yet he participated with matching vigor and rage. One night during their many quarrels, they knocked over the bassinet with the baby in it. This scared them both, but more so him. He knew he had to leave; with his infant daughter in hand, he moved out of state to reset his life. After dealing with his past, poor decisions and repercussions, he enrolled in the local community college. Now, a year later, an accountant at a large firm and a single parent of a kindergartener, he went back to school at night and fell hard for his daughter's teacher. They eventually married and yes, she is the mother of his fourth child, another girl named Grace. He could have continued in a downward spiral, he could have given up, he could have blamed others, yet he saw his actions in the fall of his infant due to his carelessness. He created a plan. He sought help. He realigned his skill set. He broke free.

You are not your past! List the things you label as shameful

I am ashamed of_____

_____

_____

_____

Now put them on a separate sheet of paper, ball it up, throw it away, burn it, or put it in your wallet as a reminder of what you are breaking free from.

Further Readings

1. Healing the Shame That Binds You, by John Bradshaw

2. Your Best You Ever: A 5-Step Plan for Achieving Your Most Important Goals by Michael Hyatt

3. I Know Why the Caged Bird Sings by Maya Angelou

Chapter 2

Don't Get Stuck Making A "Pit Stop": Self-Talk And Visualization.

Have you found yourself putting things off? I have used parenting as an excuse for one of my pit stops. The importance of this section is knowing your current mindset and how to navigate your way out. I was one of many parents that parented out of guilt. What does that look like? For me, it was a domino effect of decisions I made. So I did things to appease them in a quiet battle of their forgiveness. The silliest part is, they did not need to forgive me. They absolutely loved me unconditionally. My pit was being in the VICTIM MINDSET; I knew of the GROWTH Mindset but thought I was unworthy of being in the elite group. I was living like I did not deserve or was not in the realm of living out a growth mindset. Relationships can also be a pitstop for some; it allows you to have an excuse for not doing what you need to do for yourself and hiding behind your worth by doing for others. The problem with that is, the people you are gaging your value on don't value the emotional, social, physical and financial sacrifice because they can't see the authentic you. We ask others do they love us; the question to be asked, researched, and confirmed is do we love ourselves. Do you know the authentic you? What are you afraid of? What were your childhood dreams for yourself? I remember wanting to be a teacher, a dancer, an Olympian, a wife and a mother. These are things that should have been nurtured and invested in. I was surrounded by teachers in my family on all sides. I was an okay student who wanted to do better. In Elementary, I was the teachers' pet from K-4; in 5th grade, my teacher saw that I was not being challenged and was only being coddled; she held me to the fire two years straight. I had an awesome opportunity to be with the same teachers 1-2; 3-4; 5-6; this allowed them to see my learning style, my weaknesses, my strengths and my areas for growth; I loved my first two teachers and clung to them, it was later in life that I realized the best teacher was my 5th-6th, she did not just see the cute little girl who was well-groomed, polite, shy and had a supportive network. She saw a little black girl not being academically challenged to be the productive woman that was to come. I had the hardest time adapting to her expectations; I was faced with accountability, challenged to apply knowledge and pushed to earn every grade and opportunity; I thought I was unliked for the whole two years. I was so busy fighting to survive that I missed the learning opportunity. I do remember her asking me if I could do better and I would shrug my shoulders, and she would say, I do not know then, so show me. I read the message wrong and started my journey on proving myself worthy instead of living my truth and showing my worth. This was one of the first shovels that I picked up along the way to dig and sit in my pit stops. Now I know that I should have used the shovel to bury the self-doubt. So, the blessing of this is that you know how to talk yourself into the pit, so changing the words can get you out. I AM ENOUGH!!!!! Start with that one. Put it on a sticky note, put it as your screensaver, write it on your bathroom mirror. What are some words you use to hold you back? Write them here and now.

_____

_____

_____

_____

_____

_____

_____

_____

Replace them with I AM:

blessed, courageous, deserving, engaging, fortunate, gifted, inspiring, optimistic, passionate, unique. etc., continue with all other words that describe the best version of you now and what you want to be.

The art of self-talk is guiding the inner voice of our conscious and unconscious thoughts. The belief that we hold on to, the biases that we allow to blind us are interpreted and processed with our own words on a daily experience. I am the daughter of a broken little boy who grew up to be a man caught up in the cycle of incarceration. I am thankful that he was out long enough to be part of my conception yet haunted by the absence of his smile, gifts, and spirit. He suffered from mental illness in a time and period where our culture swept it under the rug or declared he went astray. I was directly affected by the overflow of not his gifts but his faults. A pivotal memory I have is of him walking away after a family argument and going off with friends who were not his true friends; they took advantage of his loyalty and used him as a hype man. He waved and told me he would be back; he was not. He was incarcerated for several years after that day. He left with me to bear his cross of being the daughter of a failure, a dumb ass, a waist, etc. Now how am I supposed to be proud of me, the product of the man I thought was the best thing on earth. He, my father, was my first broken heart moment that impacted my life for the next 30 years. I lived life trying to prove that I, the product of such a man, was a good person, I was smart, I was worthy. I embellished stories about my life to be more appealing than the truth. I tried to mimic what I thought was acceptable since just being me wasn't. I grew up in middle and high school in a time when light skin, good hair and thick thighs were attractive yet surface-level acceptance. I used it to my advantage at times but more than often, I wanted to have more melanin, smaller hips and thighs. I wanted to be respected for my strength, my true beauty, my intelligence. More negative self-talk took over. It's funny how people are jealous about the things you don't appreciate in yourself. I had to go back and heal the little girl of me as the adult that I became. I had to teach her to embrace her life as her own and not as a remnant of her parents, and ancestors. I was able to comfort her and assure her that I had her back at all cost and most of all, that we are okay, and we are set apart to be God's Jewels in the world. I did that by going to sleep and waking up with words of affirmation. I honed in on the Growth Mindset and understood how to recognize and balance my Inner Critic, Inner Defender and Inner Guide.

Your inner Critic is like a nagging toothache of your faults telling you that you are inadequate and sets you up for failure before you even began. Your Inner Defender screeches into a bullhorn that everyone else is the problem and blames others for your shortcomings. Your inner guide is the balance and full circle voice that seeks the best response possible with a set of actions and plans for success.

Daydreams are your creative juices flowing and the introduction to purposeful visualization. Go back to your childhood and answer the question, what did you want to be when you grew up? As I mentioned before, I wanted to be a dancer. I grew up watching Fame and attended Philadanco. I wanted to be a professional dancer and travel the world while letting my body react to guided moves and music that would touch the visual cues of the audience and tap into their emotions and memory of me every time they heard the notes. I enjoyed the challenging choreography and the creativity of moves that I could add as well. I loved the costumes and the ability to be anything I wanted to be at any given time. I miss the butterflies leading up to a recital; I miss the smell of the sweat, fear, and joy of the wooden floor of the theater as we did dress rehearsal. I revel in the noise of the crowd as they catch a glimpse of the dancers and cheer for their personal dancer. I got to relive this peaceful journey through my daughter and now niece. It is not only a time of artistic and rhythmic examples but proof that hard work pays off, that we have GRIT and determination to be what we need to be when we need to be. Yes, there are hurdles, disappointments, and bruises, but the beauty of our art is indestructible.

Take your previous success and let it assist you in visualizing what you want to be. I see myself at my 50th birthday dancing the night away to a hand-selected playlist of the decades of my life; I see the dress I want, the decorations, and the seating arrangements. I smell the fresh flowers that I have as center pieces; I hear the conversations of friends and family that are reconnecting, I feel the beat of the music, I feel the love that surrounds me, I can taste the lemon and strawberry layered cake and the aroma of the wine that is used to clink the glasses in honor of who I am at that moment.

Athletes use visualization quite often; Muhammad Ali stated on several occasions that "If my mind can conceive it and my heart can believe it – then I can achieve it." Now you put that statement to practice, you can accomplish things that will not only blow your mind but those around you. Your success will inspire others to be the best version of themselves as well.

When you begin to visualize, you need to imagine the specific situation with as many details as possible what you can see, what you smell, what you hear, what are you feeling? You can find a quiet moment and close your eyes. You can get a piece of paper and a pen to write it all down;

you can get your phone and record what you are visualizing and listen to it before you go to sleep or at any time you feel you are losing the vision. You can create a vision board electronically or on a poster board to hang for a visual reference.

What do you see in your future in the next 3 months?

_____

_____

_____

_____

_____

Tell me a scene that you see in your future (use all you're your senses)

_____

_____

_____

_____

_____

_____

Further Readings:

1. Mindset by Carol S. Dweck, Ph.D.
2. Boundaries by Cloud and Townsend
3. I thought it was just me (but it isn't) by Brene' Brown, PhD, LMSW

Chapter 3

Education Is Key, But There Are More Locks To Success.

My maternal and paternal grandmothers were both maids/nannies for doctors' families on the mainline in the greater Philadelphia area. They were vital parts in raising other children for a living while also raising their own children with a portion of the income and resources. They made sure both sets of children were clean and fed even though the quality and quantity were very drastic. They saw daily what a "Degree" could do for a lifestyle. Both were strong advocates for education; regarding school and attending college. My maternal grandmother was raised in the South and stopped attending what was considered a school for her era in the 6th grade. My paternal grandmother was raised in the North and had the ability to attend and graduate from High School. Their eyes would be bright and full of life when they saw that their grandchildren were on the honor roll, facilitated speeches, honored for academics, accepted into college, graduated from college, attended graduate school and so on. These women raised doctors as a career and in turn, created a path for their grandchildren to be on their own way to become doctors themselves. As the descendants of such women, we are blessed and appreciative, yet we learned that a degree is not the only means to success nor the remedy for poverty. We are educators who see the gaps of knowledge, the ripples of inequity and the blatant denial of access. Book smarts was a breeze for most of us, as it was an escape from the normalized dysfunction that was life. It was what we could control and what we were praised about. I, personally, was also able to use my artistic abilities and musicality as an escape. When I stopped dancing, I started playing the violin and cello. In high school, I was a student-athlete that found yet another outlet for an action that I had control over while keeping my mind busy and dreams in perspective.

What I needed to know was how to carry myself in the world not only as a woman but as a black woman. I needed to know how to respect and manage my sexuality, money, and credit score. I needed to know the ins and outs of networking; I needed to know the art of effective communication. Most importantly, I needed to know who I was and what I wanted in life. I needed to create my own definition of success. I developed a love for learning and am a Lifelong Learner. I am pursuing my doctorate degree in education to be in a position to create, facilitate and implement policy changes to educate the whole child ages birth to 18 and beyond, so we do not have to attempt to piece together broken adults who don't have the basics to living life. In my opinion, the top three things needed are EFFECTIVE COMMUNICATION, INTERDEPENDENCE and GRIT!

We need to communicate effectively by listening without the intent to rebut or respond but to understand and apply what was said. When listening, you need to be willing to understand by focusing on being intentional, being empathetic, clear on how the person feels and open to what the person thinks. You need to ask if they need your opinion or if they just need a listening ear. You remain focused. Look for body language and word cues for underlying issues that the speaker is not conveying. If in-person, sit up facing the person nodding your head in agreement within reason, over the phone, you can sound "umhumms" to assure the speaker that you are listening.

Make sure you are not assuming anything and that you repeat/rephrase what was said. You can start restating with "Sounds like; Let me be clear, what I heard you say was......" Make sure you are using your own words and not just being a recorder and stating exactly what they said. Look for nonverbal cues and behaviors such as eye contact, posture, and hand gestures. Avoid being stereotypical (Women are......). Remove judgement, be authentic and be accountable.

Now that you are an adult in this world rate what you know about the following:

Good Credit 0 1 2 3 4 5 6 7 8 9 10

Generational Wealth 0 1 2 3 4 5 6 7 8 9 10

Taxes 0 1 2 3 4 5 6 7 8 9 10

Entrepreneurship 0 1 2 3 4 5 6 7 8 9 10

Real estate 0 1 2 3 4 5 6 7 8 9 10

Debt 0 1 2 3 4 5 6 7 8 9 10

Stress Management 0 1 2 3 4 5 6 7 8 9 10

Relationships 0 1 2 3 4 5 6 7 8 9 10

If you are a parent, make sure you teach /guide your children about all the above prior to them graduating high school.

There is a misconception about being independent; I must admit that I blocked not only my blessings but those of my children trying to be "Miss Independent." I still struggle with asking for help and will weigh my options heavily. Thank GOD he has surrounded me with individuals who are like-minded. I had to take a leap of faith from the unknown. It took some retrospection and evaluation to balance dependency and being independent. I know I am not alone when I say it makes my blood boil to have anyone hold something over my head. The phrase "Oh, I had to………., "If it wasn't for me……… Oh well, you shouldn't have asked me then." It took me a long time to realize that they were hurting internally more than I was and they needed that flickering moment to make them feel better. Now, in my upright tightrope walking posture of interdependency, I can ask for help and send up a fervent prayer for anyone who attempts to hold acts of help over my head. Very few of us have become successful as totally independent individuals. You must utilize a network of skills and people to achieve your ultimate success rate. Are there unicorns out there, I am sure, yet I am not looking for them.

We are humans; we need to be in relation with each other. Just like most things in life, moderation is key. Be dependent and willing to learn in situations of growth, maturity, and exploration. This is a minimal time frame in which you are relying on someone or something else. Independence is a catalyst for isolation if not accessed appropriately. I was once told to never be alone with my own thoughts because I just could not handle the outcome. It is good to be self-reliant and capable of caring for yourself; the danger comes when you have a false sense of not needing anyone for anything. In football terms, the quarterback cannot throw to himself; he needs a receiver. He needs also to know when a scramble is necessary to get a fresh start of downs when the receiver is occupied. Interdependence has the beauty of allowing our collective skills, resources, and gifts to enhance each other while attaining success that creates a legacy.

While reading and working through the Mind portion of this book, can you look back and account for the times you continued to hit snooze?

_____

_____

_____

_____

_____

_____

_____

_____

What was the point when you reacted to your alarm, be it internal or external?

_____

_____

_____

_____

_____

_____

_____

_____

_____

Successful people without a degree

1. R. Donahue Peebles
2. Ladi Delano
3. Steve Jobs

Further Readings

1. Suze Orman's Financial Guidebook: Put the 9 Steps to Work by Suze Orman
2. It's How You Say It: Effective Business Communication Skills by Barbara Teicher
3. Making Accountable Decisions: A Journey to an Accountable Life by Sam Silverstein

BODY

(Physical, illness, respect, self-image)

Chapter 4

Listen With Your Eyes: Overcome The Reflection In The Mirror!

In 2002 I had Lasik eye surgery. I wore glasses for nearsightedness since I was in high school. I tried contacts and was not diligent in keeping them clean enough to prevent infections; I wore glasses that often were broken and rigged with tape, safety pins or glue. I was looking to embrace my face and wanted to see and show off my eyes. I was tired of looking like the homely librarian stuck in the microfiche room. Once the bandages were off and I was free of the protective shades, I was able to look not only at my face with glee but now I could see the weight that I still had after my third child. I was never an overly sensual woman (well, not in public anyway) but I was now not happy with my voluptuous figure being protected by layers of fat that had accumulated because I used food as a coping mechanism for fear, worry and celebrating. Growing up, I was ashamed of my body and was not receptive to the attention it provided me. My grandmother would insist I had shirts long enough to cover my butt; I could not wear the cute skirts in style because the bag of mine would sit higher, I had to wear my shirts on the outside of my jeans because of the rear gap due to my small waist and wide hips that the brand did not account for. Outside the house in middle school, boys wanted to play grab and run, so I had to embrace the style of wearing my jacket or Izod button-up sweater around my waist. In high school, I was defending my dignity because now I was thick, solid, curvy, athletic, light-skinned with "good hair," good grades and more male friends than most. I was not sexually active, but I was infatuated with two or three guys and although I wanted to look cute for their attention, the girls were not impressed, and I was "stepped to" daily and threatened to watch my back or be ready to protect my face. I was non confrontational, yet not an easy win if blows were encountered. The experiences that I had in those formative years led to me hiding within my body with my body. Now I was not happy with what I saw and needed to come up with a plan to reverse the damage. The most common mistake was trying to work from the outside in. I did diets, workouts, meal prep and starvation. Some pounds were shed here and there but they always came back, with friends as well. I finally realized that the key was to work inside out; I needed to figure out why I was so conscientious and ashamed; I had to deal with enjoying and embracing how GOD knit me so intricately, cell by cell. I had to learn how my body reacted to exercise, food and stress. The balance again is key to keeping all leveled.

When you look in the mirror and you do not like what you see, do not punish yourself; seek outside reflection. In the business world, managers partake in what is known as a 360 Assessment. This is an assessment that looks at how others perceive your skillset, effectiveness, and influence. You are a leader, and you need to start embracing the vision of you from those around you who are like-minded and erasing the thoughts of those who are just as fractured as you are and sadly, unable or unwilling to partake in your personal and professional growth. This is more important to those who are suppressed by family; you must acknowledge you were born in chaos to make sense of it. Let your mantra be, "It ran in my family until it ran into ME!" The process of attaining the feedback is anonymous, so it allows individuals to be truthful and not just say what they think you want to hear. The benefit is that this promotes self-awareness and can be transformational. You need to explore your personality trait, your EQ (Emotional Quotient) and your temperament.

Activity: Take some time to take the Myers Briggs Type Indicator Assessment; there are free versions online that you can take as well as seeking a consulting firm for a more in-depth assessment.

Further Reading:

1. Thanks for the Feedback: The Science and Art of Receiving Feedback Well by Douglas Stone & Sheila Heen

2. I am Every Good Thing by Derrick Barnes

3. The Gifts of Imperfection: Let go of Who You Think You're Supposed to Be and Embrace Who You Are by Brene`Brown

Chapter 5

Stop living in DEBT (Depression Exhaustion Bitterness Tolerance)

Your Credit Score is used to gauge financial responsibility; if you have good credit, you can get a car loan for 2.9% vs 12.9% . If you see the car you want and it cost, let us say $40,000 and you have good credit you can get it at 2.9% and in 5 years pay approximately $41,160 while if your credit is not in good standing, you will pay $45,160.

A difference of $4,000 over a period of 5 years that you could have saved or invested. It is the same with your body; if you are living with a bad credit score of life, you will suffer from being in more debt than you can handle.

Let's look at the acronym:

Depression can be a state of being or a clinical diagnosis. I am one who thrives off the sun, so the winter is hard for me as daylight saving time cuts my day at 4:00pm at times. I benefit from the sunlight, my body yearns for vitamin D that sunlight provides, and my mood suffers as well. I am cognizant and adjust my activities and prepare for my days with the intent of joy, prosperity, and productivity. Depression can be mild, moderate, or severe. I have experienced the symptoms of decreased energy, insomnia, and lack of interest in activities. I am aware and I make sure that my loved one's hold me accountable and encourage me to address my mood.

The DSM V categorized depression types as follows:

1. Clinical
2. Dysthymia (Persistent Depressive Disorder)
3. Postpartum Depression
4. Seasonal Depression
5. Psychotic Depression
6. Premenstrual Dysphoric Disorder
7. Disruptive Mood Dysregulation Disorder

If you feel like you or someone else may be experiencing any of the listed, please seek medical advice. (Depression Scale is at the end of the book in the appendix.)

Exhaustion while living in DEBT keeps you from being productive; it affects your internal organs as well. Your emotional exhaustion, like your body keeps you from thinking straight, keeps you in a state of stress, dries your body out as well as your will to thrive, you are short of breath and temperament, and you become a professional couch potato with no pay. Your loved ones must watch you wither away or care for you after a medical emergency such as a stroke or heart attack if they are blessed not to lose you to death. You are now forced to be dependent on those you fought so hard to be independent of. Karma is enlightening at times.

Imagine you are the spouse of a Military Officer who was called overseas for duty. You are in college to further your career, preparing for your spouse to not have to re-enlist. You have two kids actively participating in school and community sports. You are caring for your mother, who was brutally beaten by your father and your twin is on drugs, unable to cope with the physical and emotional trauma of your childhood. Your day-to-day routine is daunting, to say the least. You feel obligated to meet not only the needs of your children but their wants and desires as well. Your spouse is your confidant who you only get hours of communication with a week. Your mother's failing health is a reminder of what you were able to survive as a child and your twins' inability to cope makes you feel responsible for not saving yet another person. You refuse the help, so others are not privy to the truth under the façade you have created. It is a lovely spring morning; your mother is currently at a rehabilitation facility due to a fall. The kids are both on an overnight adventure with their friends. It is just you, the morning breeze, the chirping birds and of course, the oversized Labrador that your son begged for. Instead of a fresh cup of coffee and a relaxing moment, you are overcome with the intense urge to grasp every bit of air as you breathe in and out, your chest is tightening, and the once clear skies become harder and harder to seek. Your head is spinning, and you reach out your arms to find the back of the lawn chair to guide you to a seat. Your knees buckle and you fall to the ground. The dog is barking for you to get up to no avail. He is getting louder and louder as to call for the help you dare not want. You are on the ground pressed up against the base of the table, trying to get on your back as not to restrict your chest from expanding and retracting for the air you so desperately need and have taken for granted daily. You feel lightheaded and just need a moment to close your eyes. That moment has been interrupted by the thick tongue and peanut butter fragrant saliva of RINGO, your family pet. He has been by your side in the backyard, unable to get help for you because the 8 ft tall privacy fence does not allow anyone to see into your man-made retreat of a backyard. That day had gone, and the sun was setting. You wearily crawl up the patio stairs and make your way into the house; the backdoor has been open and unattended for hours, you fear someone could have entered while you were incapacitated, physically and emotionally. You reach for the water bottle on the counter and guzzle what seems to be the last bit of dignity you have left. You, my friend, have allowed exhaustion of your body and mind to shut you down in order to build you up. We all need to stop creating the fence around our inner world and allow others to support us; we need to delegate and prioritize not only at work to please a boss but also at home to please ourselves. What are you hiding in your backyard? What do you need help with? Who do you know you can call in this very moment to provide a simple listening ear? If you cannot make that call at this moment, get your phone or journal and list your baggage, unpack all that is weighing on you. Prioritize and delegate. You have arrived at your destination of awakening. Make the next journey intentional.

Bitterness

I don't want to spend a lot of energy on bitterness; this is dangerous and manifests in people that are detrimental to your wellbeing. This person has the mindset of being wronged and the only way to right the wrong is to hurt all who come in contact with them. Take some time to live out the following:

Activity: Get a bottle of soda and a bottle of water. The contents inside are your emotions/reactions. The outside world and people are going to attack you and rattle or shake your whole being from time to time. Now shake the bottle of soda; what happened when you finally opened it? Yes, just like the soda, you explode. Now when you shake the bottle of water, once you open it, you see the calm waters adjusting back to stillness as it was prior to being shaken with the same amount prior to opening; what are the contents of the soda, like half the amount. Don't let other people and this world disrupt and empty out your inner peace.

The stress of life could be how you react as a bottle of soda or a bottle of water. Stress can also lead you into a state of bitterness. Keep in mind these symptoms of stress and do all you need to remedy them.

Headaches	Neck and Back Pain	Fatigue
Insomnia	Irritability	Acne

Tolerance can be deceiving; it provides one with the ability to thrive & survive even when exposed to unfavorable conditions, people, and experiences. It gives a false sense of normalcy in unhealthy environments. It is defined as the capacity to endure continued subjection to something. The synonyms are also deceiving, patient, resilience, and strength. I looked at tolerance as part of me, prided myself on being strong and resilient. What I missed was the intent of my need to tolerate. I did not educate myself fully on the aspect of the word and action related to my wellbeing, my benefit, and my honor. I was too busy being and doing what was favorable to society; oh, she is so strong, she has the patience of a saint. She is so resilient; nothing will keep her down. As much as I would like to, I can't blame my father and his lack of availability; I can't blame my childhood because actually, I had a pretty good childhood. I was an adult who had navigated relationships previously, who failed to own my own wrongs and missteps in life; I wanted the Betty Croker Cake Box Mix life; add a few eggs and water. The homemade cake process was too daunting at first glance. My tolerance alarm started at the platform of the local train station. The train was late; the announcer kept updating the altered time frame. It must have been apparent that I was growing impatient because the next thing I knew, the caramelized Knight in Shining Armor shadowed my vision and asked if I was okay. Typically, when a male would approach me, I'd just give them my resting face, say nothing at all and engage in a blank staring contest. This was different; he was gentle in his words and shy in his demeanor. He showed concern and not intrigue. I spoke, he asked by direction and informed me that he was actually the engineer for the train that I was waiting for. I ended up riding the whole route with him as we chatted in between stops and route changes. It was a glorious twelve-hour excursion that led to multiple dates and outings. That all came to an abrupt halt about 3 months later when he confessed that he was married but separated, yet living in the same house with different bedrooms. Now why-o-why couldn't I read between those lines. Anyway, my level of tolerance, blinded by being patient, empathetic, understanding, and strong, catapulted me into years of disrupted inner peace with an outer shell that appeared okay.

My shell had bumps and bruises and some holes as well. I am thankful for the holes because they allowed those I trusted to see the light inside of me peeking through. It allowed them to speak, acknowledging my purpose and my beauty. It allowed them to mirror to me what they saw in me. I was able to wrangle my pride and display my dignity. It was rough at times. The heat in the oven of that Betty Croker cake became unbearable because I was created with care and ingredients that served multiple purposes. You don't have to tolerate what is not meant for you. You need to invest in yourself to know your worth. You need to fellowship and be observant of how others move. You need to embrace your intuition and muzzle the unworthiness.

Further Readings:

1. Back From the Brink: True Stories and Practical Help for Overcoming Depression and Bipolar Disorder by Graeme Cowan
2. Total Meditation: Practices in Living The Awakened Life by Deepak Chopra
3. The Power of Ritual: Turning Everyday Activities Into Soulful Practices by casper Ter Kuile

Chapter 6

Uncontrollable Growth

It's like you going to the dollar store to get a snack with a 100-dollar bill. You are so conditioned to being broke that you don't realize how to adjust. You look at the downside when the cashier tells you, "We don't take 100-dollar bills." You figure you need to suffer and miss out on the snack! Wake up; your snack is not at the dollar store? They cannot handle what you bring to the table. You are not worthless; you are too worthy. Think about the last relationship, be it familial, romantic, or platonic. What scenes are running through your head when you were trying to get a single item from that person with a bounty that was too large for them to comprehend. How many times did you dummy yourself down to meet them where they are, not to help them but to be inferior to them. Life is made of transactions, seasons, and reasons. Look at what you invest and what your return is. Be aware of the cyclical seasons and let people go as well as let people in. Be willing to understand that you may not know the reason at the moment, yet the reasons were necessary. I was watching a sermon and was entranced by 5 words that allowed me to see life in a new light. I interpreted that God will have me in a Place that allows me to understand and apply my Purpose while all along making sure I have the necessary Provisions to sustain me socially, emotionally, physically and financially. He will solidify my Identity and clearly set my Parameters. God will always put you in place to flourish while molding you to be all he has created you to be. His grace allows us to use our free will and his love disciplines us when we need to be corrected. He celebrates us with blessings beyond our imagination. Before this sermon, I was living like I only had a square footage of the area to maneuver when I was actually the owner of an acreage. Women think about a pair of shoes. Your feet are a size 9 and you have been squeezing them in size 8. You cannot go far because you can barely walk. You can't think straight because of the constant pain. So, you are inclined to be content, not moving at all.

You as an individual cannot control the growth of ill nor evil. If you allow the negativity to fester, it will affect every being of your lineage to come. You will have offspring that bare your cells and vulnerabilities. You must acknowledge that the time is now to rewrite the story of your past by fostering healing and expectation for those to come as well as yourself.

Generational trauma can become generational triumph. Generational poverty and be generational philanthropy. Step out of the confines of your zip code and expand your travels county by county until you are ready to flip the pages of your passport as you travel country by country. This may not be your physical being, yet those of your children, grandchildren, or perhaps great-grandchildren.

In sports, everyone loves the underdog; in business, everyone loves the comeback kid in life………. everyone loves the story; what is yours? Be the medical miracle and defy the odds of those who think so little of the minimal waves of brain activity of the monitor in your mind, the faint heartbeat and pulse ox reading of your body and prepare to empty out the collected particles of your broken Soul.

Further Readings:

1. Permission to Feel by Marc Brackett, Ph.D

2. The anti-anxiety diet by Ali Miller, RD, LD, CDE

3. I Really needed this today by Hoda Kotb

Soul

Chapter 7

Spring Cleaning

The winter has passed, and it is time to put the heavy clothing away that protects us from the icy sleet and blistering cold winds. We look for our bright colors and thinner coverings. We look forward to being outside and going to gatherings. In smaller spaces, we literally pack away those articles we no longer need, creating three piles: keep, discard, and donate. When we clean out our closest, we have a keep pile, a trash pile, and a think about pile. We need to do this with our lives as well. It's time to shed the outer garment of shame, defense and anger that keeps people from seeing the frame we are dealing with. What is it that you can keep? Perhaps I can be tolerant; I will keep it and tolerate the strain of change, knowing that on the other side is a horizon of opportunity. I will discard shame; my decisions of the past I will not repeat. I will throw away the victim mindset that festered the shame game. I will donate my strength by sharing my story to those currently overdressed with a protective layer that impedes them from absorbing the sun rays of warmth and agility. What are you ready to flaunt? I love my natural curl pattern and enjoy a refreshing morning shower with my wash and go ponytail that bounces freely, with a shine of great health as I take a run through the Schuylkill River Valley Trail. I go to the nail shop and deliberate on the shades of peach that I want for my pedicure as I am ready to have my toes peek out of espadrilles that I admired all winter long on the shelf in my closet.

Where are you allowing your memories to take you? I grab the broom and start to sweep in front of my door and that of my neighbors; this is a childhood memory of spending time with my grandmother. She had pride in even the entrance of her home from the outside. It was only a few feet but it was hers; it represented how she kept her home. The generosity of tending to her neighbor's door was her way of acknowledging that she knows the honor they deserve as well and that she is donating her time and energy to provide appreciation. Another catalyst to my cleaning is fresh air and music. I like to be alone when doing a deep cleaning. I used my playlist to hype my mood or inspire me to whatever I need at that moment. I open the windows as I clean out the refrigerator once again, discarding those things that have expired. The half-eaten jar of pickles carrying the biting sting of bitterness, the buttermilk that has begun to curdle with regret and finally the frozen loaf of bread for the just in case moment of despair. What are the things you are holding on to that are expired? Is it a job, relationship, or a life role? You know, a label that you have given yourself or acquired from onlookers. Keep in mind, my friend, "Labels are for cans not man."

Use the HERO in you to undress the outer layers that clothed you; describe a time when you accomplished something that seemed impossible? Go into detail:

What was the situation?

_____

_____

_____

_____

_____

What were your fears?

_____

_____

_____

_____

_____

What did you endure?

_____

_____

_____

_____

_____

_____

What was the outcome?

_____

_____

_____

_____

_____

How do you feel at this very moment?

_____

_____

_____

_____

_____

_____

Read what you wrote and circle the words that are possible strengths.

Now, use those words and share what you have learned/realized in these exercises that you can create and guide a new experience from what you now know.

_____

_____

_____

_____

_____

_____

_____

_____

Here is another activity: Find a picture of you that you like. What were you doing? Who were you with? Where were you and how did you feel?

Focus on recreating these moments of empowerment as part of your weekly routine.

Further Readings:

1. Declutter Your Mind by Marry Connor
2. Music Therapy: Discover the Healing Power of Music by Paul Catalani
3. Creative Visualization: Use the Power of Your Imagination to Create What you Want in Your Life by Shakti Gawain

Chapter 8

Unresolved Trauma: You Are Writing Your Own Book Every Day Of Your Life.

Stop running; when I stopped running, I was able to deal with the pain and grow out of it.

SAMHSA defines trauma as results from an event or series of events that is experienced by an individual as physically or emotionally harmful or threatening and has lasting adverse effects on the individuals physical, social, emotional, or spiritual well-being. How should a descendant of a white woman that once she gave birth to her mixed-race son, was stripped of her identity and classified as colored. What about the great grandchild of a man who was conceived out of rape in a time when women of color were warranted as bedwarmers and masters secrets. Imagine being the granddaughter of woman who was bartered by her father to be married off to a man who ultimately was seeking her sister. Lastly the child of a woman who felt it necessary to marry at 17 as the only means to escape poverty and farm work only to fall prey to an abusive alcoholic. How do you think the generational trauma has affected the one person who comes from the line of trauma and identity thieves? This person has low to no self-esteem, self-worth, sense of being or expectations of greatness. They see life as a victim waiting to be accosted, always on edge or defensive. Unwilling and unable to be loved yet yearning for the unconditional love that will allow them to bloom all year round. DNA is not the only thing that passes down from generation to generation. Many of our elders dealt with trauma in silence and secrecy, they never addressed it which left a sweltering stench of self-hatred and mockery. We as the new generation need to not only know our national history but the history or our bloodline. We need to research the wounds, excavate the rotten parts that have become infected. Nurture the wounds of our fallen while recognizing the patterns of destruction that maimed so many before us. As the saying goes, if you know better, you do better. You cannot know if you don't seek the knowledge. Therapy is not for the weak and weary. It is for the individual who wants the truth, who wants to be free from internal shackles and external interference. Therapy can help you uncover the thoughts, skill, blessings, and misunderstandings that you have buried under all of your protective gear. Therapy can help you communicate better with your self and those around you. What are some healthy choices you can make to provide you with therapeutic relief? I enjoy long walks on the nature trails in my area, I enjoy yoga and I especially enjoy long hot bubble baths. While indulging in my peace of mind, I am also free to have a conversation with GOD, he offers me such clarity and peace in those quiet moments. List some things you can do to release the phantom pain of past trauma in your life and those of your ancestors.

_____

_____

_____

_____

_____

_____

_____

_____

_____

Pearls are revered as the beautiful diver's jewel that went through a transformation from what was unwanted. Natural Pearls are created under pressure and coated with protective layers to allow total formation. For us, the parasite could have been abandoned, abused or neglected or simply being misunderstood. A cultured pearl goes through a similar process; I want to use it as an intentional cultivation by a Mother. She knows better and will take the time, energy, and money to hold her children to the pressure of being who they were created to be. For me and my kids, that meant I had to teach them to read not only to see but to acquire knowledge and apply it appropriately. To be involved in team sports, to be a part of the solution to society's ailments. To invest in their interest. To promote communication to share and acknowledge their feelings and embrace their individualism while shining without dimming others light. These seeds that I choose to plant in them are not for me to nourish; it was for them to do so. This journey began for them at the age of 3, when they were able to express clearly and comprehend accordingly. Were there challenges?

Yes! Is every child different? Yes. Did I have to sacrifice? Yes. Did I have to be willing to learn along the way? Yes. Did I grow weary at times, of course!

Pearls are known to provide a soothing influence, promote peacefulness and lift our spirits. I feel complete when one of my students, clients, colleagues or even a stranger tells me that I was able to make them feel better at times with a simple smile. I am a pearl.

Honesty, integrity and wisdom are more attributes of the pearl. Pearls have been associated with health implications as well; they are a source of healing physically and emotionally. Pearls have held a form of spiritual transformation as well. Looking at yourself as a Pearl or as one who wants to bring out the pearliness of a loved one taps into our being in touch with the simplicity and honesty of the things of life. You are here to provide wisdom, mirror what you want the intended to be and be satisfied in knowing that there is no need to polish to glow, for it is everlasting and undeniable.

Further Reading:

1. The Purpose Driven Life by Rick Warren
2. Permission to Feel: Unlocking the Power of Emotions to Help Our Kids, Ourselves, and Our Society Thrive by Marc Brackett
3. Grit: The Power of Passion and Perseverance by Angela Duckworth

Chapter 9

Are You Looking In A Mirror Or Through A Window?

Get out of your comfort zone; it could be holding you back. Complacency stunts growth and produces weeds. Comfort zone is where you feel safe and a false sense of control. When you are ready to step out of your comfort zone, you are hit with the FEAR zone that often causes us to retreat to our comfort zone; we know what that pain looks like there and we figured out how to tolerate it. I need you to attack fear with the simple statement: I am FEARFULLY AND WONDERFULLY MADE (Psalm 139:14). I heard in my travels that FEAR is the acronym for False Evidence Appearing Real. Let's get in the fear zone and address our lack of confidence, ignore what others think of us and remedy all of our excuses for why we can't and learn how we can…….guess what! You made it; you are now in the most important ZONE of LEARNING. Here you can look at your problems with a new lens and new skills to address them and prioritize your actions as you push and widen your comfort zone. Take your time in this zone, treat it like pregnancy, give yourself 40 weeks to give birth to your growth zone. Growing looks like you are searching and finding your purpose, setting more intentional new goals and living out your dreams ready to shine as you crawl, walk and run into your destiny.

Be real with the reflection you see in the mirror, be willing to be wrong, be willing to be accountable. In the famous fairy tale of Snow White, the Queen asks the mirror of truth who was the fairest of all; once the Queen heard the truth, she reverted to eliminating the one who was revered as the fairest. Her longing to be fairest igniting rage, fear and carelessness. She was okay with being a murderer so long as she was what she thought was the best. Why not be happy with what you see and find the specialness of yourself to have shine. Your physical attributes will only last for a time. They may be in style this year and out the next. Your inner beauty is always everlasting. Focus on your strength and enhance what you think is less than. I encountered a young woman who would rather not look at her own face. She had three sisters who were all displaying the characteristics of their father's side of the family. Thin small frame, caramel complexion and vocally were all able to sing with their soprano and alto voices. She was the middle child, second in birth two years after her eldest sister and two years older than her twin sisters. She was the mirror image of her mother. Chocolate smooth skin and she wore an ear length short bob cut. She hated her full lips and thick eyebrows that encompassed her short round face; her voice was raspy and that of a tenor to bass. She was tall and categorized a thick and curvy. She was taunted by words of her family, oh, she has childbearing hips, you sure she is not the milk man's baby and don't worry you will eventually grow into your features. She was adored by her parents, especially her father. She had minimal squabbles with her sisters. She was her worst enemy. She felt unwanted and unworthy by her image in the mirror as she compared herself to others. I remember telling her that I went to bed at night praying for more color; I loved the summer because my red undertones were now bronze glistening beams of light of my high cheekbones. I asked her what she thought she should do to make her face more appealing. With the generation she comes from, she quickly mentions plastic surgery. I told her to think about the message she would be sending to her mother. I asked her if she wanted to change her mother's features, the woman who nurtured her and celebrated her success and comforted her in her low places. She replied she never thought about it that way. People, perspectives are powerful. They allow you more insight and clarity. It took her some time, but she was able to tap into the beauty of her complexion, fuller lips, cute pudgy nose and thick eyebrows that could be shaped without being penciled in or tattooed. When you look in the mirror and think it is time for some deconstruction, you are absolutely correct, yet the deconstruction is internal not external.

My view out the window looks different when I am in different places of my life. When I was in the basement of my wholeness, all I saw were the sidewalks full of debris and the tires of the cars that were parked, some with a bright yellow boot and others flattened. One bright shiny day, I decided to go beyond my eye-level view and looked up. The sky was clear; the trees were in full bloom. It was pleasant and I wanted more. Now I look out the window and see the mountains in the far distance with green caps and roads along the hillside. I see the business of life as cars are passing, people dining outdoors, kids are playing and overcast is looming but not threatening the joys of the day. Just like me, you have the ability to change your view. Take the time to go to your window and look out.

What do you see?

_____

_____

_____

_____

_____

What do you like and or dislike about what you see?

_____

_____

_____

_____

_____

Close your eyes; what do you want to see?

Write down the three things that stood out the most in your visualization.

1. _____

2. _____

3. _____

Make sure your next move has a window that will allow you to see what you imagined.

You have the power to change your view, perspective, and way of life. It could be simple at times. It will seem impossible to others. You will have hurdles, setbacks, and success. Allow them all to build your framework for creating a better version of you daily.

Further Readings:

1. The Self-care Prescription by Robin L. Gobin PhD
2. The Mindfulness & Acceptance Workbook for Stress Reduction by Frederik Livhelm, PhD; Frank W. Bond, PhD; Daniel EK, MS; Bjorn Skoggard Hedensjo, MS
3. Five Good Minutes by Jeffrey Brantley, MD and Wendy Millstine

Chapter 10

Your Story

Forgiveness is for you, not those who have wronged you; you must also forgive yourself.

I can't give you step-by-step instructions on how to tell your story because it is just that yours. I did what I could and that was to share the skills that you need to apply as you start your travels and most importantly, a safe space to be YOU!

In this chapter, you are to start the art of journaling and write your personal journey of growth, aha moment or plan of success. GET TO IT!

_____

_____

_____

_____

_____

_____

_____

_____

_____

_____

_____

_____

Quotes to assist your journey.

Every day is a second chance.

"When obstacles arise, you change your direction to reach your goal; you do not change your decision to get there." ~Zig Ziglar

"Knowing others is intelligence; knowing yourself is true wisdom. Mastering others is strength; mastering yourself is true power." ~ Lao Tzu

Success is the sum of small efforts, repeated day in and day out. ~ Robert Collier

Know what sparks the light in you. Then use that light to illuminate the world. ~ Oprah Winfrey

"Insanity, doing the same thing over and over again and expecting different results." ~ Albert Einstein

You can't just wish for a better life; You must go out there and create it. ~ Joel Brown

If you change your mindset, you have the ability to change your whole world. ~ Damien Thomas

Affirmations to start you on your way.

I am enough.

I am part of the cure.

I am at peace with all that has happened, is happening and will happen.

I am the architect of my life; I build its foundation and choose its contents.

I am aware that GOD did not create me to float by but to ride the waves.

I will not freeze when it is time to pivot.

I will not allow fear of the unknown to keep me in my comfort zone.

Individuals to assist on your journey.

God

Accountability Partner

Mentor

Life Coach

Therapist

Psychiatrist

My Personal Reading List

1. Bible

2. Becoming

3. Hinds' feet in High Places by Hannah Hurnard

4. Boundaries

5. Relationship Goals by Michael Todd

6. The Purpose Driven Life by Rick Warren

7. Complete Guide to Money by Dave Ramsey

National Resources

National Domestic Violence Hotline

Phone: 800.799.SAFE (800.799.7233)

TTY: 800.787.3224

Video Phone Only for Deaf Callers: 206.518.9361

People They Help: Children, parents, friends, offenders

National Parent Helpline®

Phone: 855.4APARENT (855.427.2736) (available 10 a.m. to 7 p.m. PST, weekdays)

People They Help: Parents and caregivers needing emotional support and links to resources

National Human Trafficking Hotline

Phone: 888.373.7888

People They Help: Victims of human trafficking and those reporting potential trafficking situations

National Alliance on Mental Illness

Phone: 800.950.NAMI (800.950.6264) (available 10 a.m. to 6 p.m., ET weekdays)

People They Help: Individuals, families, professionals

National Center for Missing and Exploited Children

Phone: 800.THE.LOST (800.843.5678)

TTY: 800.826.7653

People They Help: Families and professionals (social services, law enforcement)

Rape, Abuse and Incest National Network (RAINN)

Phone: 800.656.HOPE (800.656.4673)

People They Help: Rape and incest victims, media, policymakers, concerned individuals

National Alcoholism and Substance Abuse Information Center

Phone: 800.784.6776

People They Help: Families, professionals, media, policymakers, concerned individuals

National Suicide Prevention Lifeline

Phone: 800.273.TALK (800.273.8255)

TTY: 800.799.4TTY (800.799.4889)

People They Help: Families, concerned individuals

National Runaway Switchboard

Phone: 800.RUNAWAY (800.786.2929)

People They Help: Runaway and homeless youth, families

Attachments:

❖ Quick Inventory of Depressive Symptomatology (QIDS SR-16)

Source:

https://loricalabresemd.com/wpcontent/uploads/2017/12/qids-

sr16.pdf

❖ SMART GOALS. (I am thinking about making this a perforated colorful sheet)

➢ Specific – be clear and specific, so your goals are easier to achieve; this will help you understand how and where to get started.

➢ Measurable – make sure your goal can be tracked so you can see your progress as you work towards completion.

➢ Active/Attainable – you should be taking action to achieve your goal by taking steps that you are committed to. They can be challenging to improve your growth, yet not impeding.

➢ Realistic- you want your goals to be achievable, fun, and rewarding. DO not make them stressful and frustrating.

➢ Timebound – Create dates and deadlines for each step. This will help you stay focused, motivated and proud.

Acknowledgements of Supporters

My triple threat Eric, Briana and Miles

Siblings

Parents

Bloodline; my family

Heart strings; my villagers who are more like family than just friends.

I am publicly acknowledging my first 10 supporters who purchased my book in a flash:

Syieda Graham

Christi Fox

Janet Carr

Shelley McDonnough

Paul Hogue

Claire Graser

Dawn Mobely

Sheila Bryan

Jantra Stone

Stacey Henry-Carr

You all collectively represent my family, my childhood, my transition to adulthood, my professional life, my parenting stage, my faith system, my emerging friendship, my acocuntatblity and my future. What an awesome collection of wholeness I received in you showing up in support of me.

Bio

Erica Evans was educated in the public-school systems of Pennsylvania by way of The School District of Philadelphia (West) and The William Penn School District (Delaware County). She saw it fit to become an educator herself by way of profession in Early Childhood, K to 12 and Higher Education. Today she is an active advocate for Early Childhood education and equitable access to high quality childcare for she believes birth to five are the most formative years in a child's life and educational pathway. She is currently working As an Advisor for a virtual platform for students and families in Kindergarten through their Senior year of high school. She is an Adjunct Instructor at a local Community College in the surrounding Philadelphia Area. Over the past 25 years she has come to realize the Education is not just about the ABC's and 123's it is about Insight, Intuition and Immersion.

Her life-long Learning mindset, exposure to excellent clinicians as an administrator in behavioral health and her passion for access led her to share the path of recognizing the sound of her own alarms, her unwillingness to head and just hit snooze. Her alarms were blaring in the way of parenting, relationship management, self-esteem and old scripts.

This book was created to work your inner muscles of self-love, to be able to stretch your arms of self-reflection and stop reaching for the snooze button and start reaching further for the pen to chart your own journey of awakening. This book is an appetizer to the four-course meal you are preparing to nourish yourself and your legacy for generations to come.

Made in the USA
Columbia, SC
09 June 2024

36427146R00043